Motivational Phrases

for All of

LIFE'S
CHALLENGES!

K. J. Roberts

ISBN: 978-1-4269-9523-1 (sc)
ISBN: 978-1-4269-9524-8 (e)

Library of Congress Control Number: 2011916410

Trafford rev. 09/19/2011

 www.trafford.com

North America & international
toll-free: 1 888 232 4444 (USA & Canada)
phone: 250 383 6864 ✦ fax: 812 355 4082

To Mary Roberts and Donna Hargrave

If not now- when?

If not here-where?

———————

The task ahead of us
Is never as great as
The power behind us.

———————

You can tell how big
A person is
By what it takes to
Discourage them!

We grow the most
As a result
Of surviving the
Darkest of times!

It's not supposed to be easy –
If it was – everyone would
Be doing it.

———————

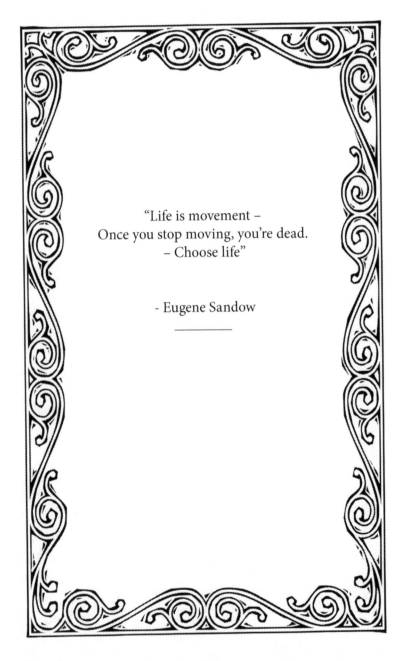

"Life is movement –
Once you stop moving, you're dead.
– Choose life"

- Eugene Sandow

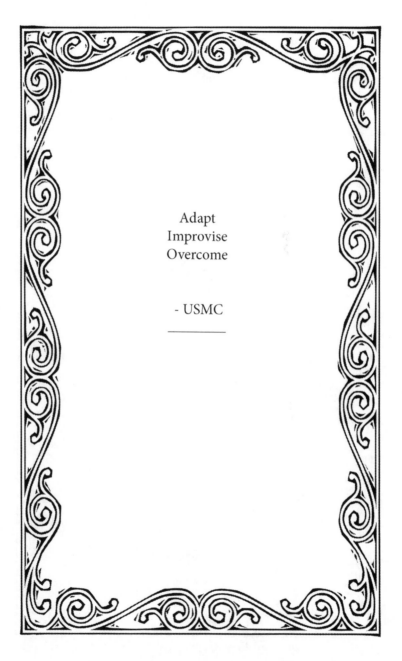

Adapt
Improvise
Overcome

- USMC

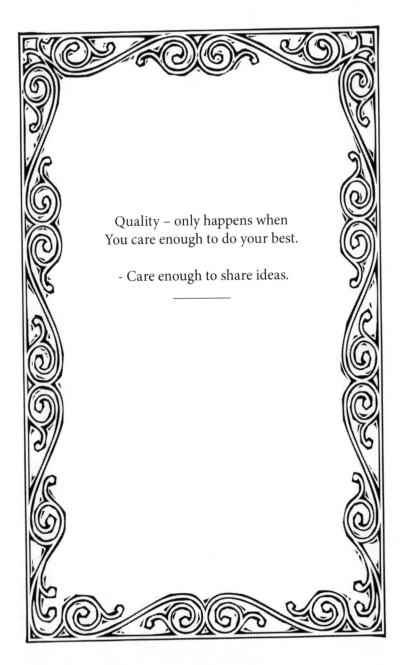

Quality – only happens when
You care enough to do your best.

- Care enough to share ideas.

———————

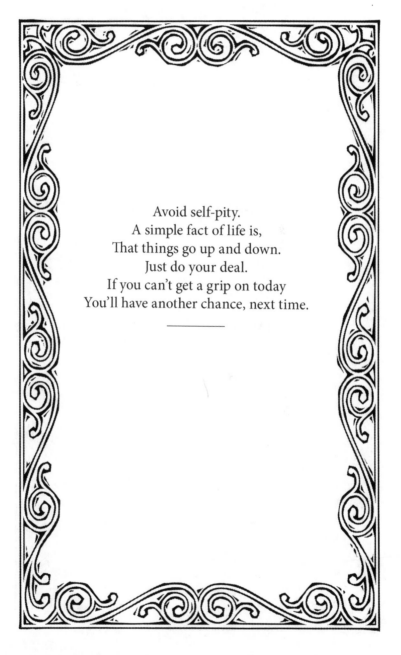

Avoid self-pity.
A simple fact of life is,
That things go up and down.
Just do your deal.
If you can't get a grip on today
You'll have another chance, next time.

———

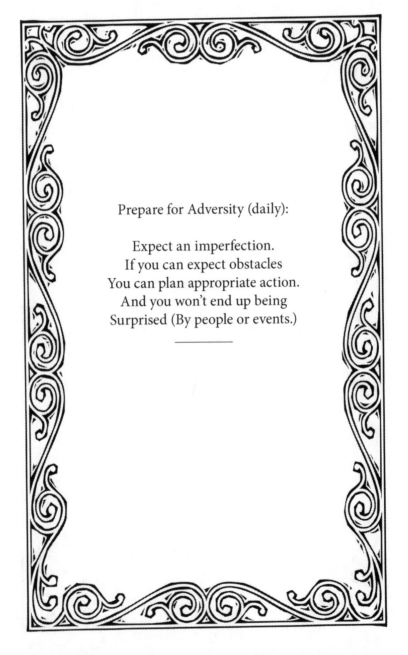

Prepare for Adversity (daily):

Expect an imperfection.
If you can expect obstacles
You can plan appropriate action.
And you won't end up being
Surprised (By people or events.)

———————

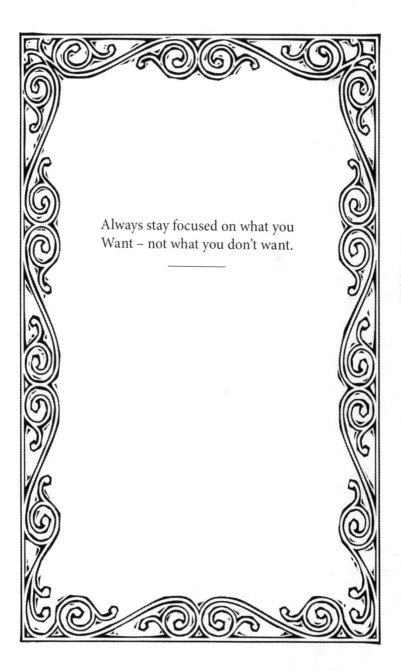

Always stay focused on what you
Want – not what you don't want.

———

"Ask yourself: 'what do I want?
What is important to me?'"

———

"Think about: The person you wannabe
The life you wanna live
- This creates the life you want."

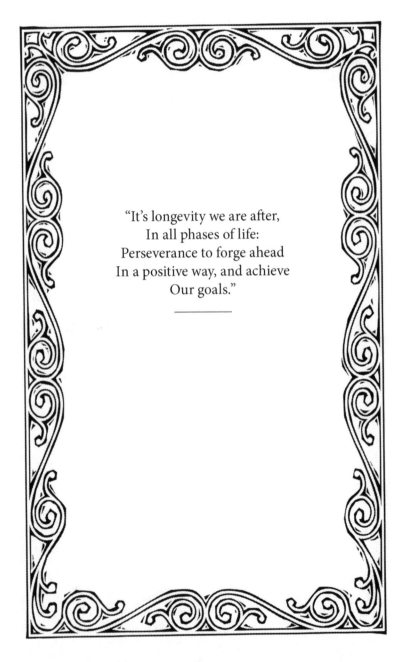

"It's longevity we are after,
In all phases of life:
Perseverance to forge ahead
In a positive way, and achieve
Our goals."

———————

"Walk the walk –
Don't talk the talk."

———————

Hang in there when it
Becomes difficult

———

What could I do today
That I know would take a
Lot of effort?

———————

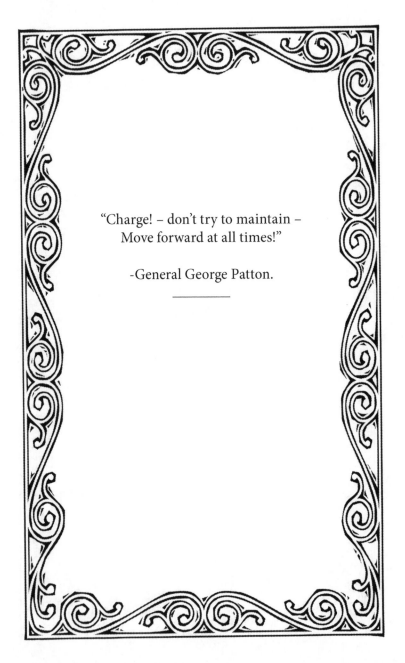

"Charge! – don't try to maintain –
Move forward at all times!"

-General George Patton.

———————

"Challenge me –
Doubt me
Disrespect me
Tell me I'm older
Tell me I can no longer fly!
- I want you to."

- Michael Jordan

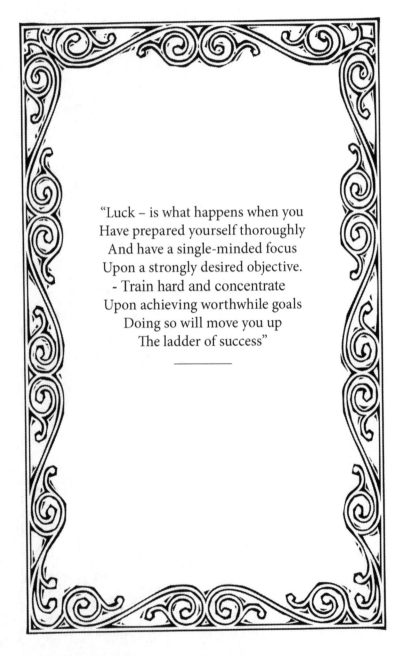

"Luck – is what happens when you
Have prepared yourself thoroughly
And have a single-minded focus
Upon a strongly desired objective.
- Train hard and concentrate
Upon achieving worthwhile goals
Doing so will move you up
The ladder of success"

Set small, achievable,
Sensible goals.

———————

Work for quality
Not quantity.

———————

A great plan
Not followed –
Yields poor results

———————

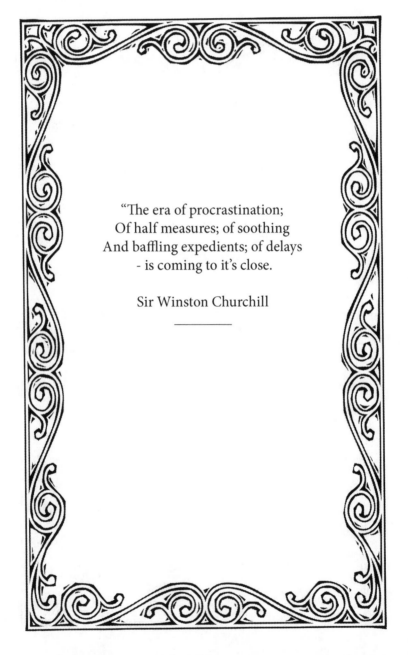

"The era of procrastination;
Of half measures; of soothing
And baffling expedients; of delays
- is coming to it's close.

Sir Winston Churchill

———————

Old tigers, sensing their end,
Are most fierce, and go down,
Fighting!

———————

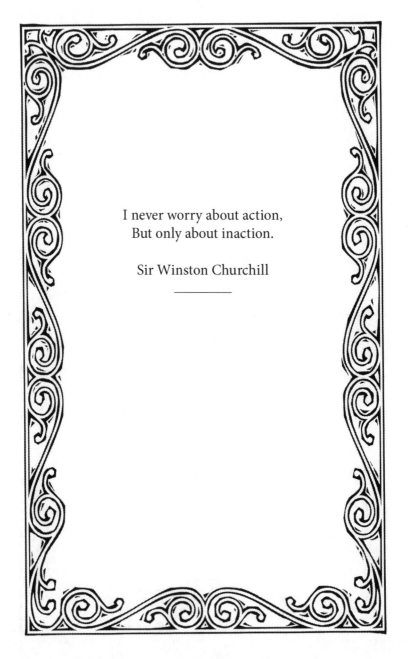

I never worry about action,
But only about inaction.

Sir Winston Churchill

———

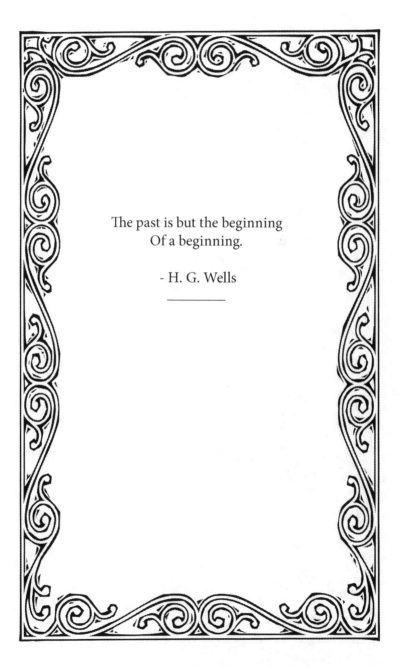

The past is but the beginning
Of a beginning.

- H. G. Wells

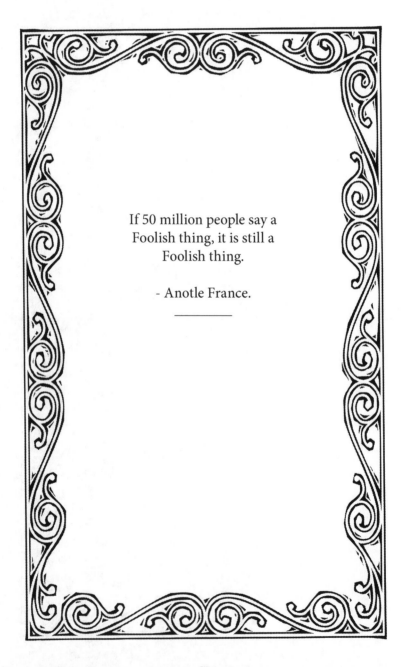

If 50 million people say a
Foolish thing, it is still a
Foolish thing.

- Anotle France.

———

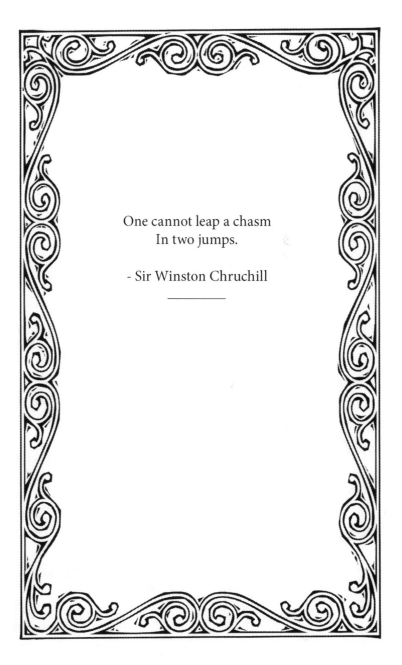

One cannot leap a chasm
In two jumps.

- Sir Winston Chruchill

———————

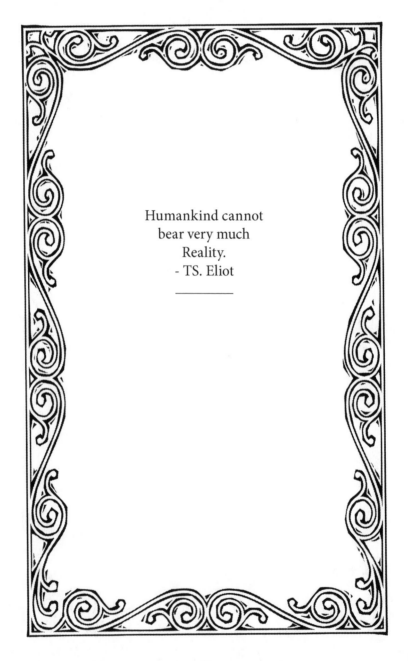

Humankind cannot
bear very much
Reality.
- TS. Eliot

_____

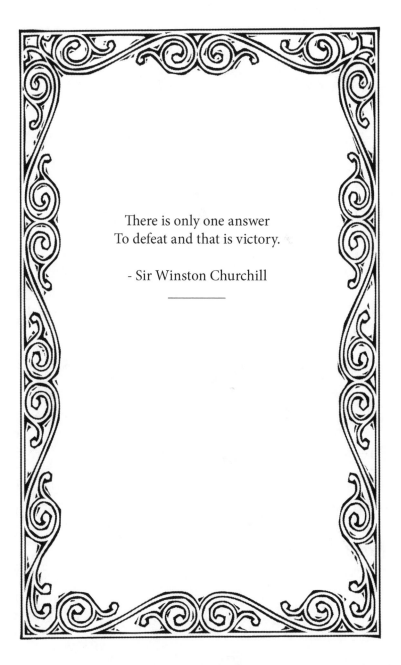

There is only one answer
To defeat and that is victory.

- Sir Winston Churchill

———————

Each AM puts a man on trial
And each PM passes judgment.

- Roy L. Smith

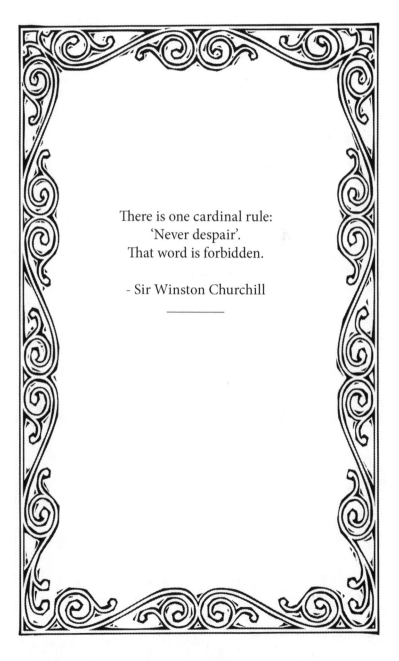

There is one cardinal rule:
'Never despair'.
That word is forbidden.

- Sir Winston Churchill

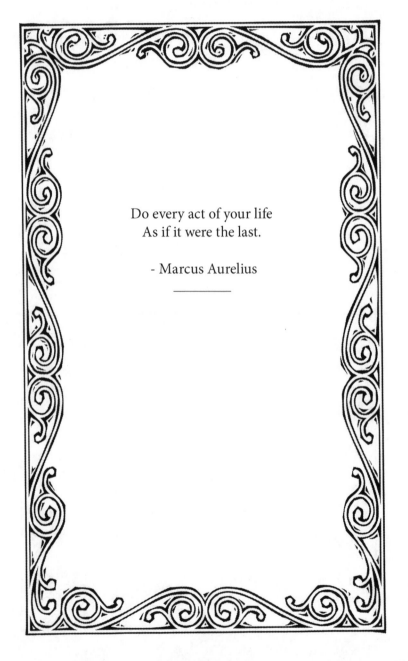

Do every act of your life
As if it were the last.

- Marcus Aurelius

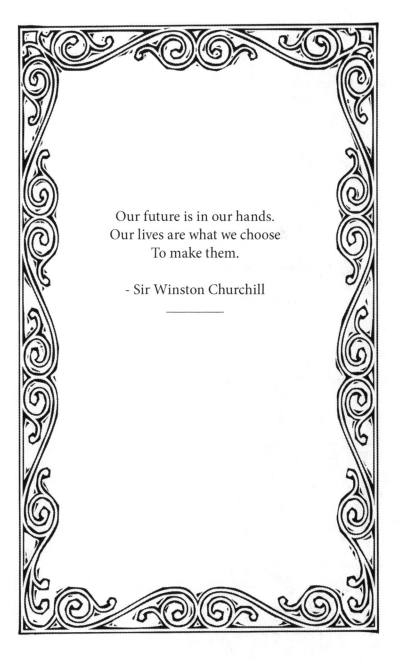

Our future is in our hands.
Our lives are what we choose
To make them.

- Sir Winston Churchill

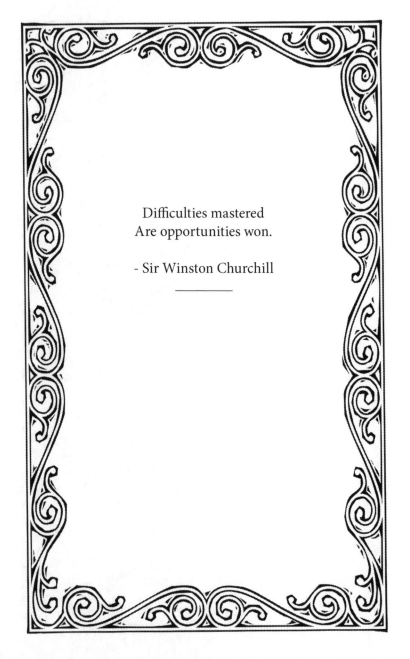

Difficulties mastered
Are opportunities won.

- Sir Winston Churchill
———————

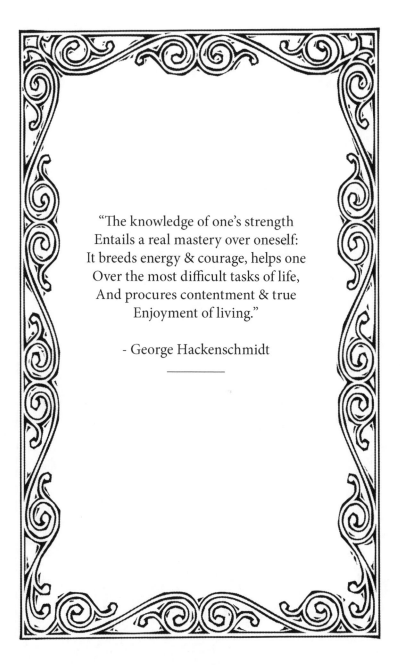

"The knowledge of one's strength
Entails a real mastery over oneself:
It breeds energy & courage, helps one
Over the most difficult tasks of life,
And procures contentment & true
Enjoyment of living."

- George Hackenschmidt

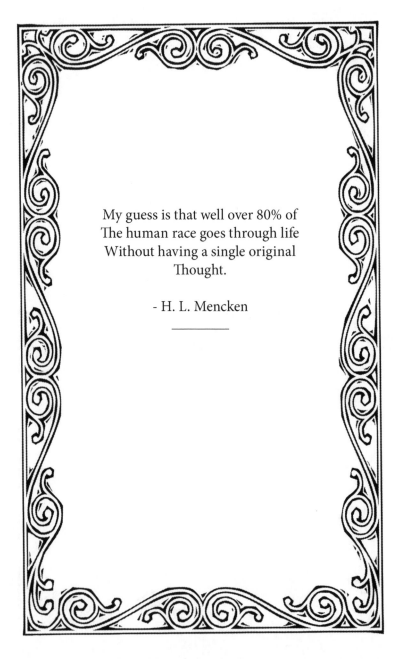

My guess is that well over 80% of
The human race goes through life
Without having a single original
Thought.

- H. L. Mencken

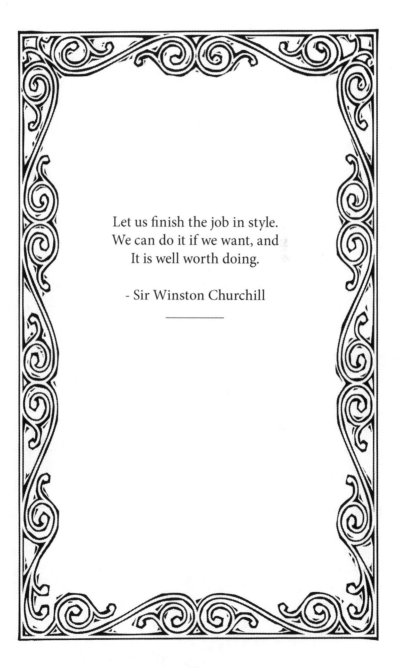

Let us finish the job in style.
We can do it if we want, and
It is well worth doing.

- Sir Winston Churchill

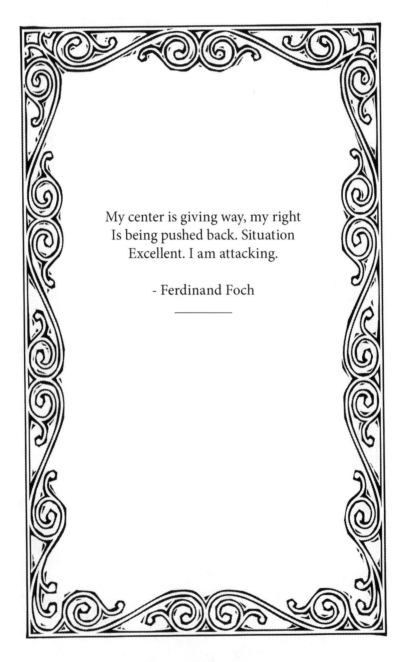

My center is giving way, my right
Is being pushed back. Situation
Excellent. I am attacking.

- Ferdinand Foch

———————

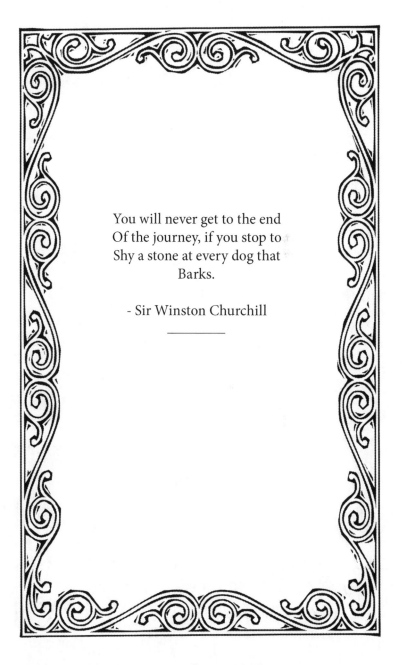

You will never get to the end
Of the journey, if you stop to
Shy a stone at every dog that
Barks.

- Sir Winston Churchill

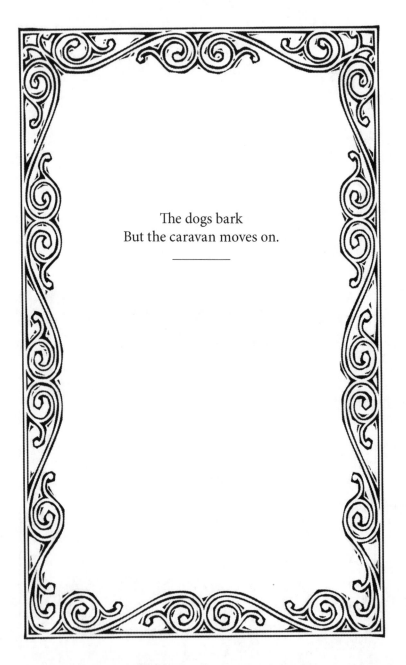

The dogs bark
But the caravan moves on.

———

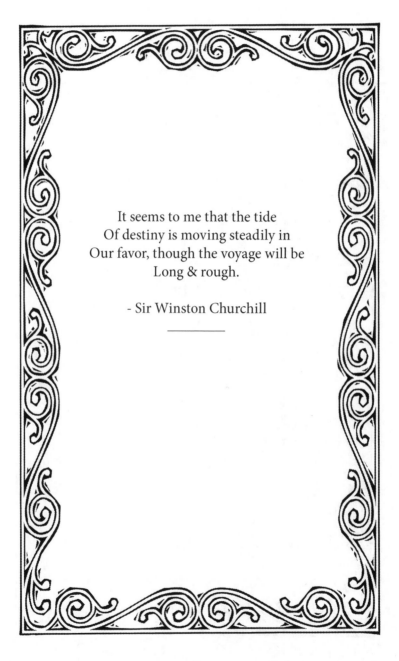

It seems to me that the tide
Of destiny is moving steadily in
Our favor, though the voyage will be
Long & rough.

- Sir Winston Churchill

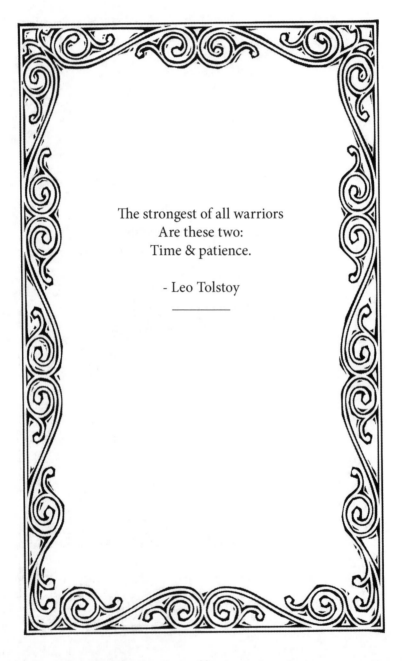

The strongest of all warriors
Are these two:
Time & patience.

- Leo Tolstoy

———

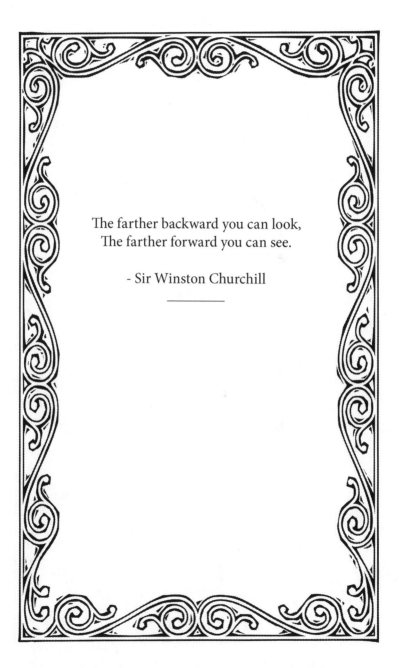

The farther backward you can look,
The farther forward you can see.

- Sir Winston Churchill

———

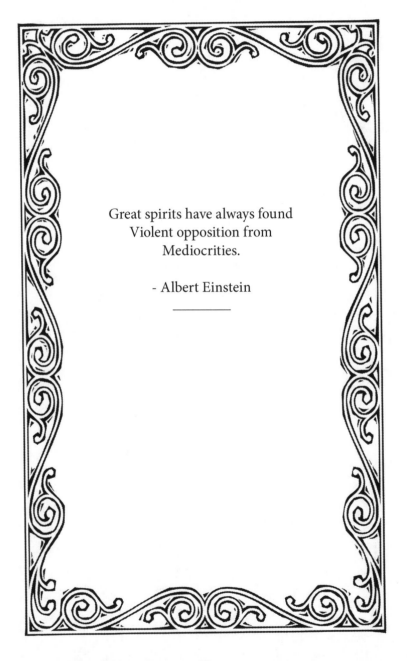

Great spirits have always found
Violent opposition from
Mediocrities.

- Albert Einstein
_____

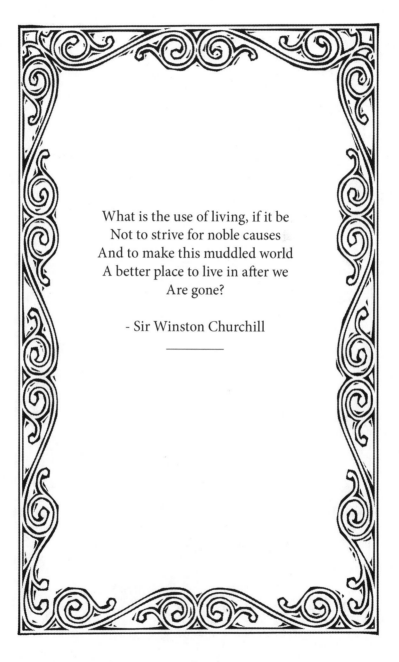

What is the use of living, if it be
Not to strive for noble causes
And to make this muddled world
A better place to live in after we
Are gone?

- Sir Winston Churchill

———————

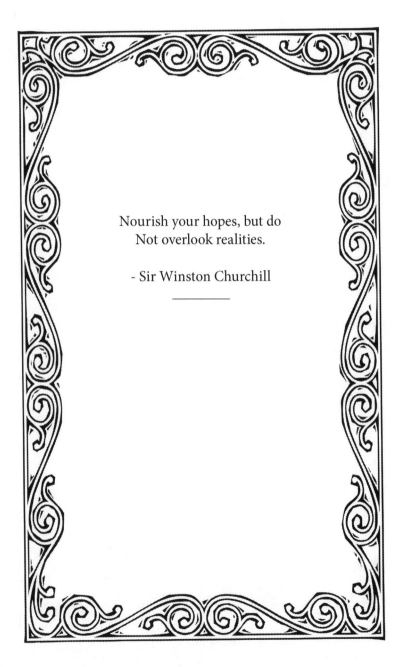

Nourish your hopes, but do
Not overlook realities.

- Sir Winston Churchill

———————

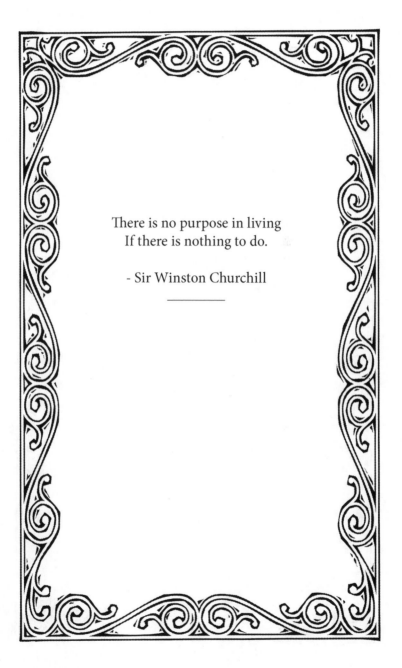

There is no purpose in living
If there is nothing to do.

- Sir Winston Churchill

———

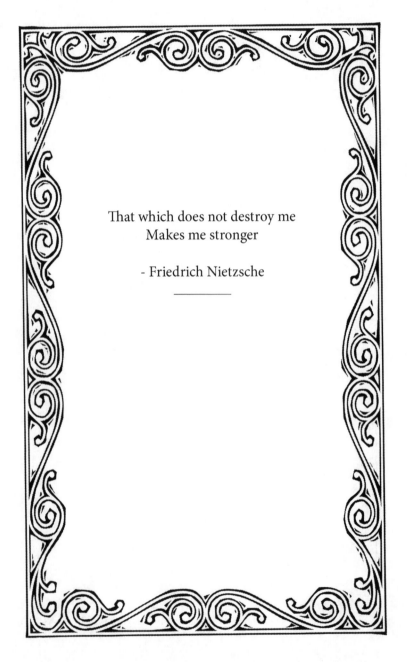

That which does not destroy me
Makes me stronger

- Friedrich Nietzsche

_____

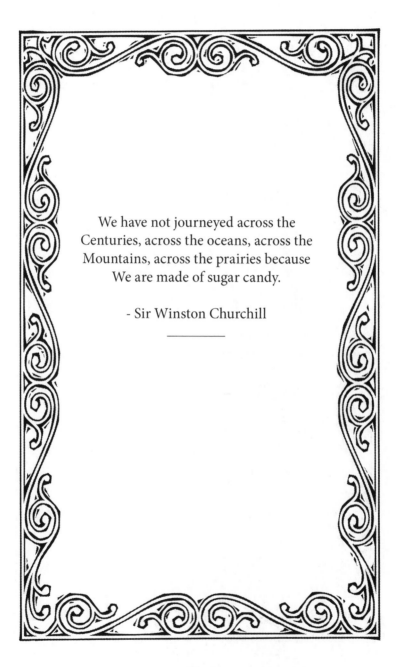

We have not journeyed across the
Centuries, across the oceans, across the
Mountains, across the prairies because
We are made of sugar candy.

- Sir Winston Churchill

———————

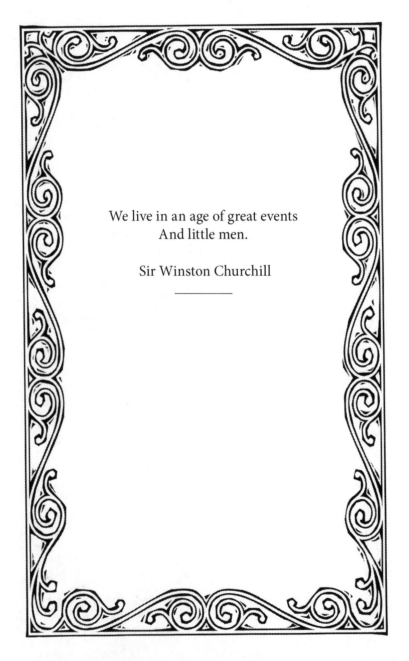

We live in an age of great events
And little men.

Sir Winston Churchill

———————

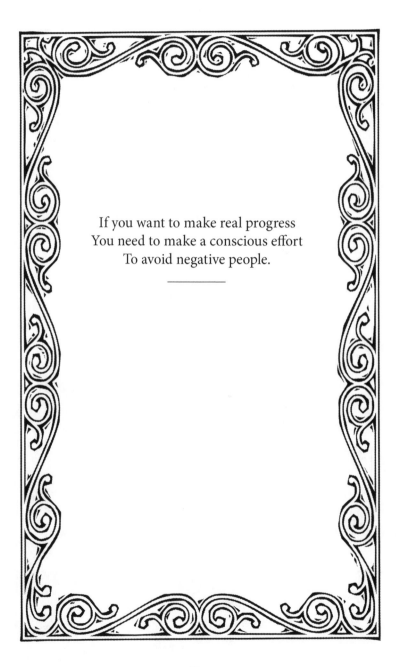

If you want to make real progress
You need to make a conscious effort
To avoid negative people.

———————

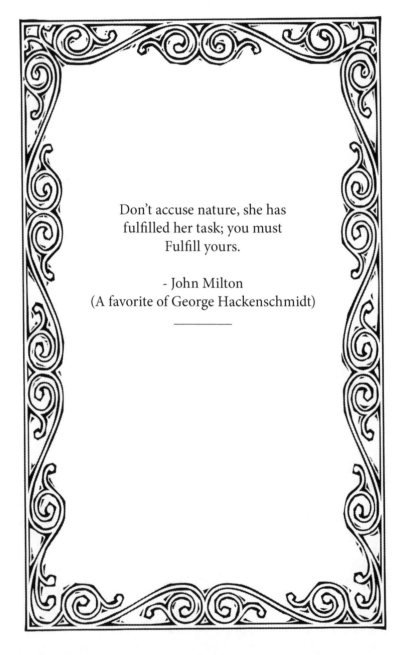

Don't accuse nature, she has
fulfilled her task; you must
Fulfill yours.

- John Milton
(A favorite of George Hackenschmidt)

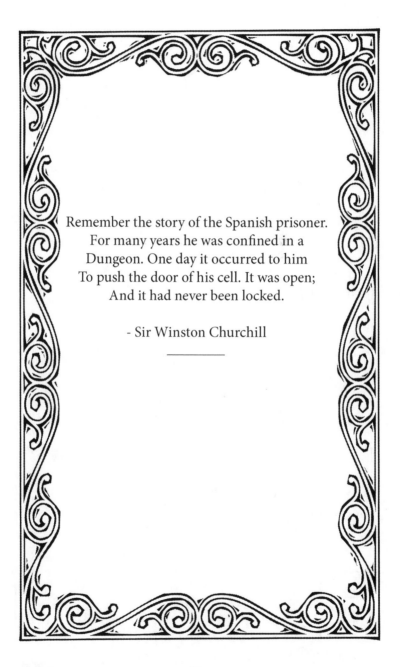

Remember the story of the Spanish prisoner.
For many years he was confined in a
Dungeon. One day it occurred to him
To push the door of his cell. It was open;
And it had never been locked.

- Sir Winston Churchill

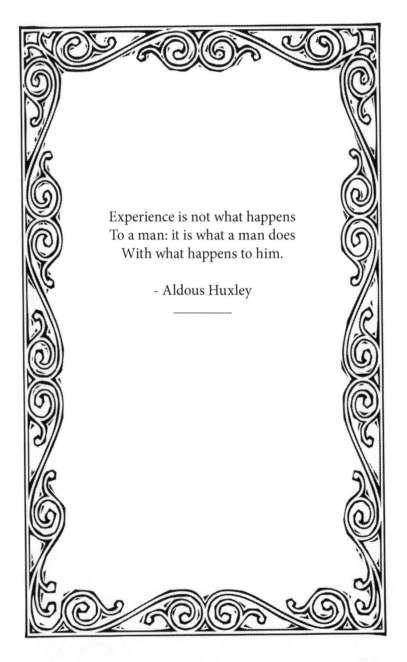

Experience is not what happens
To a man: it is what a man does
With what happens to him.

- Aldous Huxley

"Never flinch,
Never weary,
Never despair."

- Sir Winston Churchill

———————

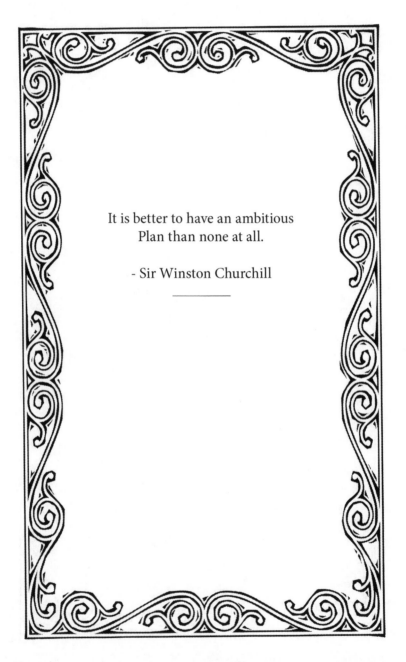

It is better to have an ambitious
Plan than none at all.

- Sir Winston Churchill

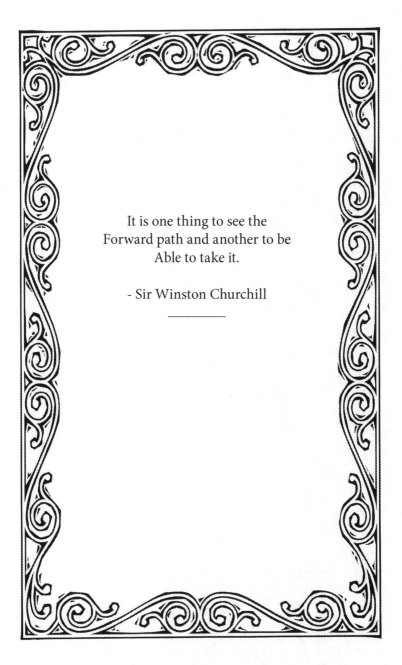

It is one thing to see the
Forward path and another to be
Able to take it.

- Sir Winston Churchill

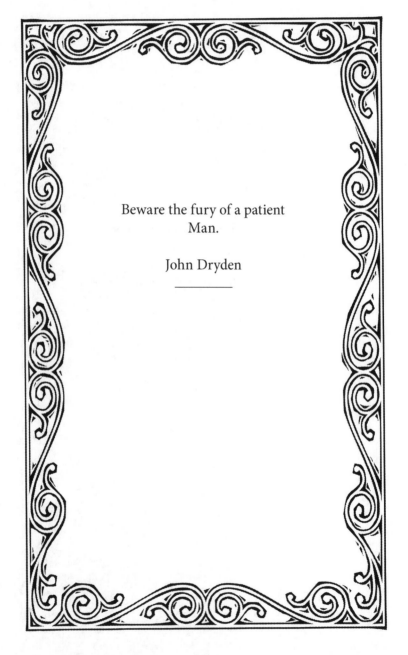

Beware the fury of a patient
Man.

John Dryden

———————

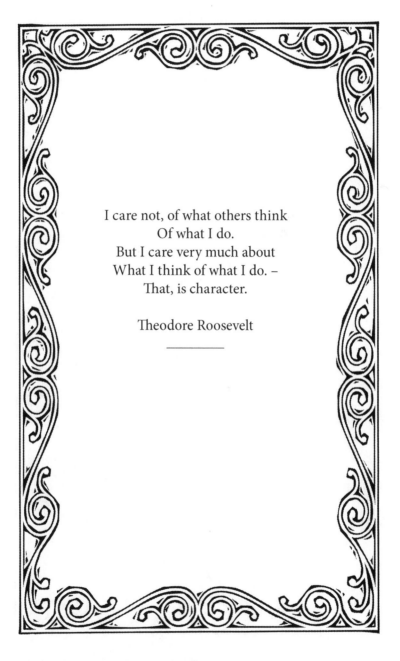

I care not, of what others think
Of what I do.
But I care very much about
What I think of what I do. –
That, is character.

Theodore Roosevelt

_____

"Keep breathing; tomorrow the sun
Will shine – and there's no telling
What the tide will bring."

- From 'Castaway' Tom Hanks

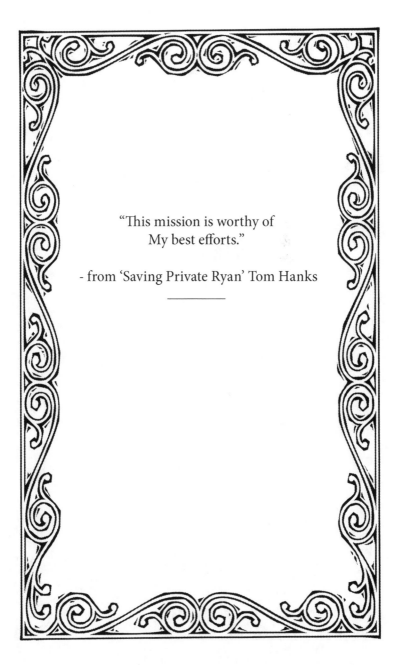

"This mission is worthy of
My best efforts."

- from 'Saving Private Ryan' Tom Hanks

'Where there's a will
There's a way.'

———

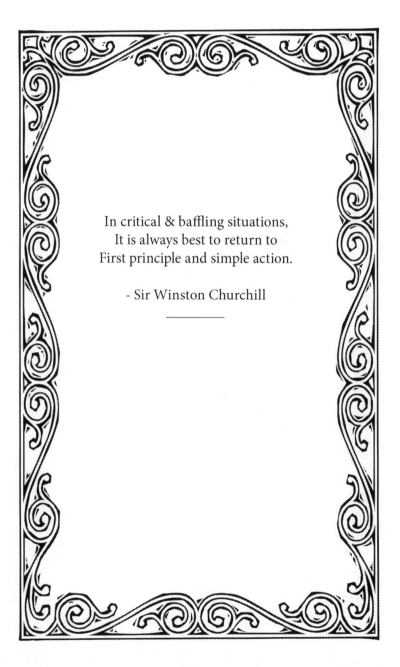

In critical & baffling situations,
It is always best to return to
First principle and simple action.

- Sir Winston Churchill

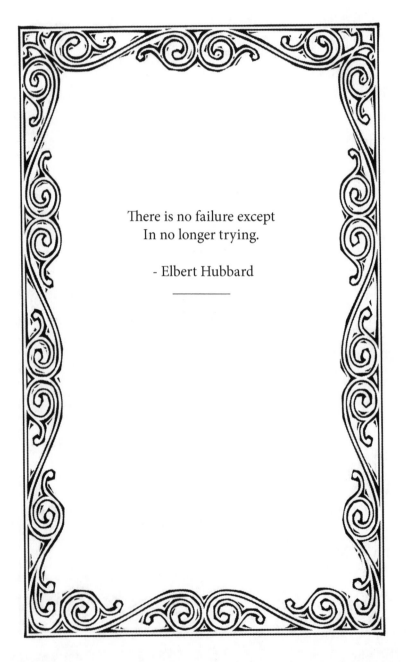

There is no failure except
In no longer trying.

- Elbert Hubbard

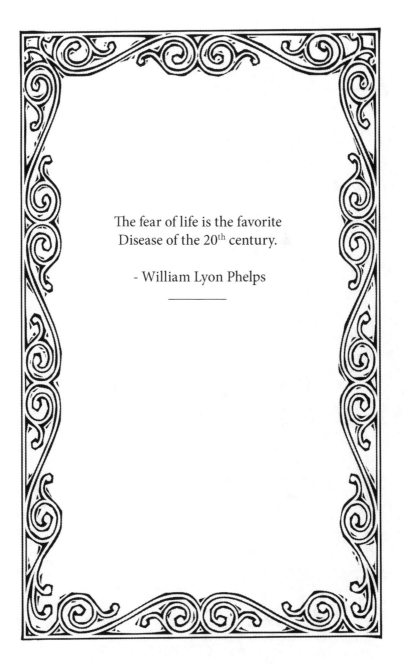

The fear of life is the favorite
Disease of the 20th century.

- William Lyon Phelps

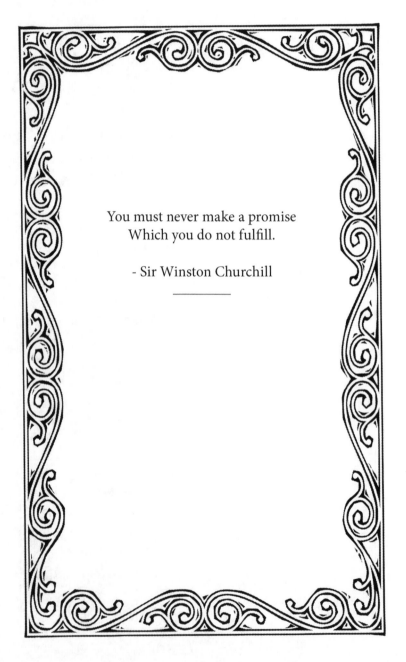

You must never make a promise
Which you do not fulfill.

- Sir Winston Churchill
_____

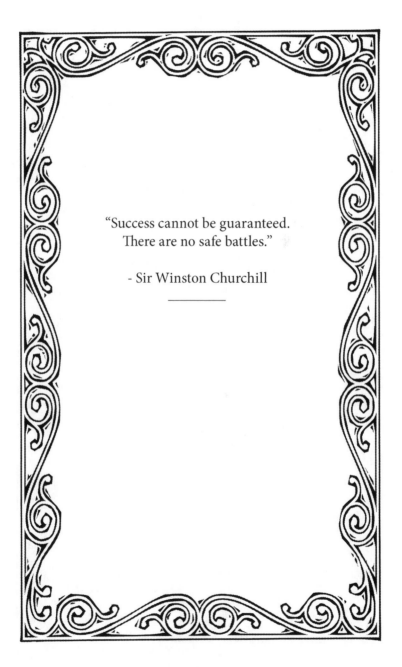

"Success cannot be guaranteed.
There are no safe battles."

- Sir Winston Churchill

———————

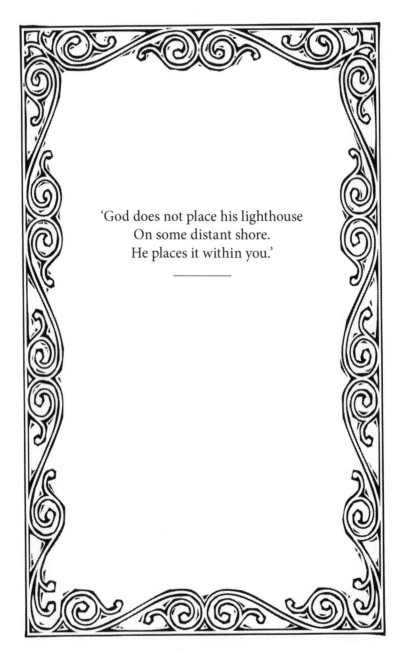

'God does not place his lighthouse
On some distant shore.
He places it within you.'

———————

- It is a light that never
Dims or flickers – penetrating
The deepest part of your heart,
With truth, love, and life'

———————

"God never muses in our
Moment of need.
He is ever present, moved with
Compassion, and sovereign in his
Provision"

———————